21st Century
Junior Library

DISCOVER THE ALLOSAURUS

Lucia Raatma

**Our Prehistoric World:
Dinosaurs**

Published in the United States of America by:

CHERRY LAKE PRESS
2395 South Huron Parkway, Suite 200, Ann Arbor, Michigan 48104
www.cherrylakepress.com

Content Adviser: Gregory M. Erickson, PhD, Dinosaur Paleontologist, Department of Biological
Science, Florida State University, Tallahassee, Florida

Reading Adviser: Marla Conn, ReadAbility, Inc.

Photo and Illustration Credits: Cover, page 12: © MattLphotography/Shutterstock.com; pages 5, 18:
© Image Source/Alamy; page 6: © Marysha/Shutterstock.com; page 7: © Lord Beard/Shutterstock.com;
page 9: © Eye Risk/Alamy; page 10: © Noiel/Shutterstock.com; page 11 top: © Universal Images Group
Limited/Alamy; page 11 bottom: © Rob Wilson/Shutterstock.com; page 13: © Steve Bower/Shutterstock.com;
page 14: © STT0006463/Media Bakery; page 17: © Daniel Eskridge/Shutterstock.com; page 20: © Nine_
Tomorrows/Shutterstock.com; page 21: © Danny Ye/Shutterstock.com

Cherry Lake Press is an imprint of Cherry Lake Publishing Group.

Library of Congress Cataloging-in-Publication Data has been filed and is available at catalog.loc.gov.

Cherry Lake Press would like to acknowledge the work of the Partnership for 21st Century Learning, a Network
of Battelle for Kids. Please visit http://www.battelleforkids.org/networks/p21 for more information.

Printed in the United States of America
Corporate Graphics

Note from publisher: Websites change regularly, and their future contents are outside of our control.
Supervise children when conducting any recommended online searches for extended learning opportunities.

CONTENTS

WHAT WAS AN ALLOSAURUS?

Imagine being a young dinosaur living in an ancient forest. A big, meat-eating dinosaur is chasing you! It might be an *Allosaurus*. This powerful **predator** lived about 150 million years ago. Like other dinosaurs, the *Allosaurus* is now **extinct**.

A hungry *Allosaurus* was a dangerous animal.

Where did the name *Allosaurus* come from? It is a word that means "different lizard." Why did scientists choose that name? It's because the *Allosaurus* had features like no other dinosaur. The *Allosaurus* lived in western North America. *Allosaurus* fossils have also been found in Germany and Tanzania.

Allosaurus lived in what is now the United States.

Think!

When you think about dinosaurs, what do you picture? Do you see a gentle animal eating plants? Or do you imagine a scary creature with big, sharp teeth?

WHAT DID AN ALLOSAURUS LOOK LIKE?

The *Allosaurus* had powerful legs and short arms. Each hand had three fingers. Each finger had a claw. A claw could be as long as 11 inches (28 centimeters). This dinosaur had a bulky body and a big tail.

The *Allosaurus* had large, strong legs.

6 feet
(1.8 meters)

40 feet (12 meters)

This fierce dinosaur was about 38 feet
(11.6 meters) long and as tall as 16.5 feet (5 m).
Most *Allosauruses* weighed between 1 and 3 tons
(.9 and 2.7 tonnes). That is about as heavy as a car.

An *Allosaurus* was about as long as a school bus.

The *Allosaurus* was a fierce fighter with its sharp teeth and claws.

12

The *Allosaurus* had heavy bones. Its thick neck was shaped like an S. Its skull was about 3 feet (1 m) long. There were bony ridges above each eye. Its jaws were strong. It had 70 sharp teeth that were 2 to 4 inches (5 to 10 cm) long.

Look!

Pay attention next time you are in a hardware store. Look at the nails. The *Allosaurus* had teeth as long and sharp as some nails!

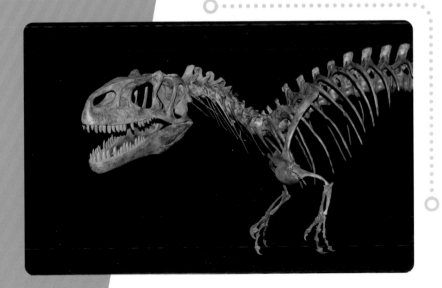

An *Allosaurus* could hunt dinosaurs that were larger than it was.

HOW DID AN ALLOSAURUS LIVE?

The *Allosaurus* was a dangerous carnivore. It hunted and ate other dinosaurs. It used its powerful jaws and sharp teeth. The huge *Stegosaurus* and *Apatosaurus* were some of its prey. The *Allosaurus* may also have scavenged for dead or dying animals.

You may wonder how the *Allosaurus* could hunt larger dinosaurs. This predator likely hunted in **herds**. A group of *Allosauruses* could corner a large *Stegosaurus* and attack it. Even a big dinosaur could not defend itself against an *Allosaurus* herd.

Ask Questions!

Talk to your friends and family. Do they feel stronger and safer in a group? Do any of them prefer not to go out alone? Imagine why the *Allosaurus* hunted in groups.

This herd travels and hunts together.

17

Allosaurus sprinted faster than the dinosaurs it hunted.

The *Allosaurus* was a fast runner. Its **stride** was about 9 feet (3 m) long. Scientists believe that it could run 21 miles per hour (33.8 kilometers per hour). That's as fast as a car driving down the street! Other estimates say *Allosaurus* could run as fast as 34 miles per hour (54.7 kph) in short bursts.

All *Allosauruses* are extinct. How do we know about the *Allosaurus*? Scientists study fossils. Many of these fossils were discovered in Colorado and Utah in the United States. Scientists are still learning about this large, dangerous animal. What will they find out next? Will you be the one to discover it?

Scientists who study fossils are called paleontologists.

Create!

Ask an adult for a box of toothpicks and some glue. Try making a small dinosaur skeleton with these materials. Now think about scientists assembling dinosaur fossils. How hard do you think it is to do this?

GLOSSARY

carnivore (KAHR-nuh-vor) an animal that eats meat

extinct (ek-STINGKT) describing a type of plant or animal that has completely died out

fossils (FAH-suhlz) the preserved remains of living things from thousands or millions of years ago

herds (HURDZ) large groups of animals

predator (PRED-uh-tur) an animal that lives by hunting other animals for food

prey (PRAY) an animal that is hunted by other animals for food

stride (STRIDE) the length between an animal's feet when it walks or runs

FIND OUT MORE

Books

Braun, Dieter. *Dictionary of Dinosaurs: An Illustrated A to Z of Every Dinosaur Ever Discovered.* New York, NY: Chartwell Books, 2022.

Rockwood, Leigh. *Allosaurus.* New York, NY: PowerKids Press, 2012.

Websites

With an adult, learn more online with these suggested searches.

Denver Museum of Nature & Science: Prehistoric Journey

Travel through time and watch *Allosaurus* and *Stegosaurus* in battle.

San Diego Natural History Museum: Fossil Mysteries

Learn about the dinosaur fossils on display.

INDEX

ABOUT THE AUTHOR

Lucia Raatma has written dozens of books for young readers. She and her family live in the Tampa Bay area of Florida. They enjoy looking at the dinosaur fossils at the local science museum.